others to enable and encourage the potential of young people. We don't have all the answers but we have fun trying, and encourage an action research perspective to testing and evidencing what works.

All these activities have been successfully tried and tested in a classroom somewhere near you!

❝Emblazon these words on your mind… learning is most effective when it's fun.❞

Peter Kline

❝To learn anything fast and effectively you have to see it, hear it, feel it.❞

Tony Stockwell

Concept

Wow! What power I have!

Our brains are amazing and exploring something about them can be very motivating for learners. Research into the brain is amassing at an incredible rate, but we have to be *very careful* about using this research for learning at the moment. There have been lots of statistics bandied about regarding how much of our brain we use, for instance the myth that we use only 10 per cent of our brain. The reality is, we don't know.

However, it is generally believed that we underestimate the potential we have, and sometimes we fail to inspire children with a sense of awe and wonder about their own potential. Thinking about the brain is good fun and can help young people realize that they have more potential than they are using. If learning is to be fun it is also important that we understand how we are affected by what we eat and drink, the amount of sleep we get, our stress and the brain's response to different stimuli.

Sessions in which students learn about the brain introduce them to the power they have in their heads. If students are excited and amazed at their brain's own potential, they are likely to understand how to learn more efficiently as a result. At birth, only a third of brain cells are connected – the rest are just waiting for brains to be stimulated by new learning. We then go through a processing of 'pruning' out cells in the brain, and this can go on well into our twenties. The general principle seems to be – use it or lose it.

There is so much that we still don't know, and new findings continue to excite and amaze us. But some signposts from science give credence to what good teachers have always known: every child is capable of achieving success.

Making learning fun has a lot to do with the self-motivation of learners. There are a lot of ways of engaging learning through understanding our strengths and weaknesses as learners. One of the fun ways into this is to marvel at the power of our brains and to shift our metaphors of intelligence.

Application

- Give one student the number 1 and tell them to stand at the front of the class. One by one, students holding up 0s come out to join them. Tell the class to put up their hands as soon as they think the number is the number of neurons (brain cells) the average person has at birth. Stop when the number reaches 100,000,000,000 – one hundred billion. Alternatively, stick 1 and about 20 noughts around the room and tell the students to go and stand next to the number they think is correct, or give groups the digits and tell them to make up the number they guess. Afterwards, tell the students that, when neurons are stimulated, they connect together, and if we keep stimulating them we can keep strengthening the connections.

- Imagine the room is a giant brain and each student is a brain cell (neuron). Ask about a third of the students to stand up and 'connect' with each other in some way, for example, holding hands miming sending an electronic pulse to each other or saying the word 'connecting'. Now ask the rest of the class to stand up and get everyone connected to each other – can they see the difference? If you've asked the students to talk to each other to show the connections, you'll hear the difference too.

- Extension: the older the students the more amazing facts they should accumulate. Ask them in teams to out 'amaze' each other by researching the power of the brain and displaying this research on posters. Another extension of this would be for older students to impress younger ones with a demonstration of some of these findings.

Concept

What the brain needs

We all know that good athletes have to be fit. They have to eat well, sleep well and practise hard. To learn well you need to look after your brain.

You can improve your brainpower by:

- Getting plenty of sleep. Your brain needs time to sort out information that has come in during the day.

- Drinking lots of water. Dehydration can lead to headaches and tiredness. Water does not mean tea, coffee or fizzy drinks…it means pure H_2O.

- Eating a balanced diet. Plenty of 'brain food' like fish and green vegetables really does help.

- Exercise in general helps enormously; your brain uses up to 20 per cent of your total oxygen intake. Regular aerobic exercise is therefore very important. It also improves your mood and is helpful when you are stressed.

- Avoiding too much chocolate, coffee, sugar, fizzy drinks, foods with E numbers and alcohol. They are bad for your brain because they interfere with messages being passed from one cell to another.

Application

The **Learning Rucksack** is a useful introductory activity, but works just as well as a review activity – it's also great to do in assembly. The activity helps students to develop their own 'toolkit for learning'. In the rucksack are some of the things that are important for learning, based on our understanding of the brain.

Invite volunteers to come up, feel inside the rucksack and take something out. They stay at the front of the group, holding the item they have taken out. Ask the volunteer, or other members of the class, to explain what they think the object represents. Put the following items in the rucksack:

- **Bananas** These are especially good brain food.
- **Bottle of water** Hydrating the brain is essential for smart learning.
- **CD** Music can help us to learn.
- **Colour chart/pack of felt pens** The brain loves colour. When we need to remember something, using colour to underline and emphasize it will help.
- **Map** We need to know where we are going; we need to set goals. The brain likes to be given the big picture of what we are learning and why we are learning it.
- **Length of rope** Our brain is a social brain and needs to communicate with and talk to other brains. Use two volunteers to hold on to either end of the rope.

- **Large cut-out smile** This signifies a positive outlook and attitude. If you tell your brain to do something it is more likely to be able to do it than if it thinks it can't.
- **Pillow** Sleep is important for learning.
- **Camera** Your brain loves pictures and can recognize up to 35,000 images an hour.
- **Trainer** Movement is good for learning and it is important to take regular exercise.

Concept

Multiple intelligences

According to Professor Howard Gardner, we all have at least eight different ways of being intelligent. He uses the word intelligence deliberately in order to contrast with our old views of intelligence. It's important to be aware that a range of intelligences are likely to be represented in any group. Don't slavishly try to provide different activities for each intelligence in every lesson. Make sure that, over a topic or programme of work, all the intelligences are catered for, preferably with tasks that involve more than one intelligence area.

Not all researchers agree with Howard Gardner, but young people find it highly motivating to think of themselves as smart in different ways when often they have been told, or internalize the message, that they are stupid. Exploring the metaphor of multiple intelligences is a fun learning to learn activity. It can help learners think about where they might use their strengths in a fun way to work on a difficult piece of learning – for example, making up a rap about some maths work.

The intelligences Gardner identifies are:

- Interpersonal
- Intrapersonal
- Mathematical/Logical
- Musical
- Naturalistic
- Linguistic
- Kinesthetic
- Visual/Spatial

Remember that everyone has a combination of all eight intelligences, though some will be stronger than others, and very few people rely on just their main one. According to Gardner, all the intelligences can be developed, so offering activities which cover a range of intelligences will give students a chance to try out and develop those they do not rely on.

Application

Here are some examples of multiple intelligence activities.

French Song/Rap
Students make a list of 20 French words they need to learn. They then choose a tune they like and compose a song or rap including all these words; they can use English as well and they should spell out some of the French words. When they know it off by heart, they should perform it to the rest of the class.

History or Geography Story
Students list the keywords in a history or geography topic. If the order is important, for example, chronological order, they should keep the words in that order. Students then write a story including all the keywords; it should be as funny, sad or ridiculous as possible. When they have highlighted all the keywords, they should read out the story, performing an action to represent each keyword.

Music or Technology Jigsaw
Students make a list of keywords and write a definition for each. They write the words and definitions onto card, adding illustrations and using colour, then cut up the cards to make a jigsaw, in which the words are separated from their definitions. Swap the jigsaws around and see how quickly other students can put them together.

Maths Cards
Each student needs four cards. On each of the four sides of the cards, students write:

- a rule or method they need to know
- an example question that needs the method to solve it
- four or five other questions they have made up themselves
- the answers to those questions.

They should use colours and cartoons on the cards to make them more memorable. Mix up all the cards and see if other students can match the questions to the method and answers to the questions.

English Street
(For a novel) Students list the characters in a novel and write some key points about each. They think of their own street and imagine characters living in some of the houses (family groups should live together), then draw a plan of the street, indicating who lives where. They should then visualize themselves walking down the street and meeting each character in turn. Can also be done for a collection of poems.

Concept

Identifying multiple intelligences

Even though no one depends on just one of the eight intelligences, everyone wants to know which is his or her main intelligence – and it's fun finding out. It's useful for individuals to know which intelligence they favour, and helpful for a teacher to know which intelligences predominate in any group they are teaching. Remember, however, that intelligences can change as we develop new competences, so the nature of individuals and groups can alter very quickly. Also, though it's important to play to our strengths, we should not exclusively stick to activities that relate to our main intelligences; trying to use the ones we do not favour can help to develop them.

There are a number of tests available that you could use to identify your own and your students' main intelligences. Some can be found on the internet. Most work on the principle of responding to statements like 'I like to learn by listening to other people.' or 'When I listen to music I can pick out individual instruments.' either by scoring them on a scale of 1 to 5 or by agreeing or disagreeing.

Tests like these offer a snapshot of the subjects' intelligences at a particular moment in time; responses are very subjective and might change from day to day, depending on activities the subjects have enjoyed or disliked. Also, the statements can't cover all the subtleties of each intelligence. However, they are fun and can be done quickly. It's best to do them in the context of discussion about multiple intelligences. Begin by looking at a selection of images of famous people, past and present; discuss in what ways they are or were intelligent.

Application

Multiple Intelligences Run Around

Another way of asking young people to reflect on intelligence strengths is to give students simple tasks and ask them which ones they felt most/least comfortable with. Set out the tasks as a series of workstations and send the students, in groups, to begin at different ones, then progress to the next after a fixed period of time. Giving a short time can help to sharpen the students' reflections on how they approached a task.

Some tasks might be:

Interpersonal – Look at some pictures of scenes in which people are in conflict; suggest what the problem might be and how it could be resolved, or role-play the scene and bring it to a resolution.

Intrapersonal – Imagine you were a castaway on a desert island, and write your diary entry for one day. (This could be done orally.)

Mathematical/Logical – A selection of mathematical puzzles.

Musical – Listen to a recording of instrumental music. Identify the instruments playing and try to give the piece a title.

Naturalistic – Sort a pack of cards with pictures of plants and animals into what you think are appropriate categories.

Linguistic – See how many words you can make from a long word such as 'PHOTOSYNTHESIS'.

Kinesthetic – Identify a selection of objects in a 'feely box' from touch alone.

Visual/Spatial – Spot the differences in two almost identical pictures, or find a hidden object in the room using a sketch map.

Human Bar Chart

Put posters representing each intelligence along one wall. When students have tried all the activities and identified their main intelligences, they should stand in front of the poster they think represents them best.

Concept

My learning strengths and weaknesses

We can have more fun learning when we understand what we're good at and what our frustration points might be. Raising awareness of our strengths and weaknesses as learners allows us to think about how to work with these qualities, or work around them. These qualities could be about learning styles or personalities but not necessarily. There are a lot of questionnaires about learning styles out there and there is a lot of doubtful practice around. The research seems to suggest we should be very careful about how we use learning styles. However, it is worth just getting learners to think about this for themselves and it can be done in a fun and active way.

> **TIP:**
> Don't start relabelling students with learning styles, for example 'oh he's a kinesthetic learner'. It just gives another limiting belief and there is little evidence that identifying someone in that way improves your teaching. The trick is for learners to understand the complexity of their learning for themselves and then work with their understandings to constantly improve.

Application

Stand Up and Change Places If…

This game is played with students seated in a circle. A statement is read out, and if people agree with it or think it applies to them they stand up and quickly change places with someone else in the circle. This is an energetic and quick way of reviewing ideas and makes a good icebreaker.

For this concept the statements could be things like:

Stand up and change places

… if you like making things with your hands
… if you have difficulty finishing tasks
… if you like to have music on when you work
… if you prefer to work on your own
… if you like to get stuck straight into a problem
… if you like to know why you are doing something (see the big picture)
… if you find note taking difficult
… if it helps you to make a mind map.

A number of statements could be made up about study skills and preferences so that both teacher and student can see areas that might need coaching. Mix things up with fun statements such as 'if you love x pop group' or 'football team'.

Dream it.
Believe it.
Do it!

Concept

I believe

There is some very good research now about the power of positive self-talk and how we can limit our potential through negative beliefs. A lot of 'pop' psychology makes it sound easier than it is and sometimes failure and difficulty are essential for successful learning. The point is how we 'orientate' ourselves towards learning and how we deal with difficulty.

Fun and motivation are increased if we can understand, challenge and re-sculpt our self-talk. That little voice in our heads can be put to good use! Building up habits is very important and we have to encourage ourselves and students to have fun with their self-talk.

All people who are world-class in their sport, art or work have got there because they practised so much more than anyone else – again, well-evidenced research!

Application

Inspiring stories

This activity looks at an example of how amazing positive thinking can be. The following summary of Cliff Young's story can be read to the class in order to get the children thinking about positive thinking and to stimulate group discussion:

> Cliff Young was 61 years old when he decided to enter one of the longest, most physically challenging marathons in the world. The Sydney to Melbourne race is around 600 km long and takes about five days. A sheep farmer all his life with no racing experience, he had no idea how long the marathon would take. He simply went for it. He was competing with some of the world's fittest athletes, but took first place – nine hours ahead of the second-place runner!

> How did Cliff manage to win. He wasn't an athlete, he had no special equipment, he had no marathon training. Talk in groups and come up with some qualities Cliff must have had. What sort of person was he?

Cliff thought he could do it; everyone else thought he was mad. Did he let what other people thought of him stop him? He believed he could and he felt he could.

- ■ What can we learn from Cliff?
- ■ How might this help with your learning?
- ■ Are there other stories that you could collect of people who 'beat the odds'?

(The main point here is that because Cliff hadn't run the race before, he had no preconceived ideas or limiting beliefs about it. Cliff won because he kept running, no one told him that everyone else slept. On the farm he was used to chasing after sheep all night or running from storms. When he entered the race the media thought he was crazy and would die!)

Concept

I believe – what's in it for me?

Although we need to avoid having really unrealistic and over-optimistic views about what we can do, Cliff Young's story (see p15) illustrates how limiting others' views of us can be. But our own self-talk can be very limiting. If we think something is going to be really boring then unless we do something about approaching it differently then we will make it really boring. A lot of good psychological research is showing us how we can alter our self-talk and how learning can be more fun if we work on a positive outlook. However, some things are hard to do and sometimes we need to fail in order to learn better.

When faced with a hard bit of learning, think longer term about why it could be important and what it will do for you. And fix on long-term goals to work through the difficulties.

TIP:
Resource material ('Challenging my thoughts!') can be found on p129 of *Let's Learn How to Learn* (see p96).

Application

Challenging Your Beliefs

This is designed to encourage students to challenge any limiting self-belief about schoolwork by thinking about their motivation to do it.

Make up a sheet of between 20 and 30 statements that you might say when doing a piece of work. Have a mixture of positive and negative ones, for example:

- 'I can do it.'   • 'I don't want to do it.'   • 'Great!'

- 'It's boring.'   • 'I will enjoy this.'   • 'I'm scared.'

- 'It might be difficult.'   • 'I really love doing this.'

- 'I think I'll have a go.'   • 'I hate this sort of thing.'

Ask students to think of three pieces of work: one they enjoy, one they don't like and a piece they feel is pointless. Using a different colour for each piece of work, the students underline statements that describe their feelings about each piece then look at the negative/positive self-talk.

In order to get yourself motivated try to:

- think, 'Why do I want to do this?'

- think long term: 'What will it help me to do?'

- listen to what your inner voice is saying. When you think about it, are you really saying 'I can't' or 'I won't'? How can you challenge your own inner voice about this thing?

- Imagine doing something in the present and attach a strong emotion to it. For example, 'I am enjoying succeeding in my work.' Thinking of the future, for example, 'I will do…' gives you permission to put it off!

If you think carefully about why you need to do this thing, you'll probably come up with a good reason. Once you have, you'll be much more likely to have a positive mental attitude towards it.

Make a promise to yourself that you are going to change what your inner voice is saying about this. Tell someone what it is that you're going to try to change – perhaps a friend, your teacher or someone at home.

Concept

How am I feeling right now?

Often when we enter a new learning situation or come into a familiar class, we still have a number of feelings buzzing around our heads that we might or might not be aware of. Sometimes these feelings can stop us from enjoying the learning or concentrating fully. There are some useful habits we can use to help 'park' these feelings, or at least help us re-frame ourselves a little towards the learning, and they can be fun things to do. Like anything else if we're constantly asked about our feelings we tend to withdraw or become very shallow in our response, so this part of the review is just a 'quick tap' into our intuitive and unconscious processes. Neuroscience research has clearly demonstrated the importance of hunches and intuition and emotional re-framing in order to plan and learn from complex tasks.

> **TIP:**
> Use the *Big Book of Blobs* by Pip Wilson and Ian Long for reviews and feelings work; there's about 60 pages of photocopiable ideas using 'Blob' figures: www.blobtree.com.

Application

What am I feeling right now?

Have a range of landscape photographs around the room depicting lots of different types of landscapes. Ask students to walk around and choose one they can identify with their feelings. Ask a few volunteers why they chose that one. If this is difficult at first, model the idea for the students.

For example, I chose the beach with the crashing waves because I feel a bit uncertain, like the waves crashing on the beach. No one has to reveal what they feel but ask them to visualize the landscape and how it matches their emotions. If their landscape matched negative emotions ask them to then choose another that they could imagine being happier or more secure in.

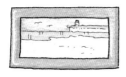

Concept

Temperature check

As thinking and feeling are so interwoven, it is very important to get students to express feelings about learning, not just regurgitate the content of a lesson. There are some fun ways to do this and they can be used as 'temperature checks' through the course of a lesson or at the end of a session. Do them regularly as quickfire habits using different metaphors each time to help engage young people in identifying with the processes of learning and therefore helping to bind the knowledge to their memories. The process can start quite simply with a temperature check about their understanding of the lesson, for example, marking out where they feel they are on a large picture of a thermometer. So that hot represents really understand to very cold – haven't got a clue! The application on p21 looks at extending this using metaphor.

Application

The 'If I Were...' Review

The 'Temperature check' can be usefully extended to reviewing a lesson or learning topic. In this application suggest a category such as a musical instrument, piece of fruit or an animal and then get them to complete the sentence 'If I were a musical instrument I would be...' as a way of describing how they feel about their learning. For example one student said 'I would be an electric guitar because I feel jingly-jangly and excited', another said 'if I were an animal I would be a lion because I was a roaring success' and another said 'if I were a piece of fruit I would be an orange because when you peel me I have lots of bits of learning inside'. Once students become more practised at this, start to ask them to expand their phrases so that they include a feeling referring directly to something they have learned in the session.

You must review your learning regularly.

Team motivation

2

Concept

Icebreakers, finding names out

When you meet a group for the first time, or when you are working with a group who are new to each other, or are about to engage on a new topic that requires some co-operation, it's important that you all get to know each other as quickly as possible. It's difficult for learning to take place efficiently if students are anxious and worried about who they are going to be working with, so 'Getting to Know You' activities are important. Often, just learning each other's names helps to put students at ease. A group feeling built through fun activities also increases motivation and energy to learn. Names are important and respect for each other helps making learning situations more engaging. Research as many name games as you can to provide variety.

Some students will be reluctant to join in, no matter how much fun the icebreakers are. Look out for them and give them your support. Joining in yourself often encourages reluctant participants. It's best not to put too much pressure on students who are shy or withdrawn. You may want to go on from icebreakers to further team building activities particularly if the group has come together for a specific task.

Learning is a social activity, and while not everyone will always get on with each other we cannot learn without a significant degree of co-operation and interaction. Working with others can be made fun and motivating and that will in turn impact upon students' self-development as learners.

Application

Here are some 'getting to know your name' starters.

Group Juggle
Participants stand in a circle. Everyone says his or her name out loud. The leader says someone's name and throws a koosh ball (or something else soft) to them. The person who receives the koosh ball throws it to somebody else and says their name as they do so. Keep going until everybody has thrown the ball. Nobody must throw or catch the ball more than once. It is important to remember who you threw to and who threw it to you. Go round again, throwing to the same person as before. After a while, the leader throws in another koosh ball, which must go round in the same pattern. See how many koosh balls you can keep going at the same time. Encourage the students to throw the ball low and soft, because powerful throws will send the ball out of the circle and hold up the game.

Name/Adjective/Action
Students introduce themselves with their name and an adjective starting with the same letter, for example, small Sally, happy Habib. Make it more fun by adding an action for the adjective. To make it harder, ask volunteers to recall all names and adjectives at the end.

Say Your Name
Sitting in a circle, each student says his or her name in turn. They say them in a variety of ways, for example, fast or slow, high and squeaky, low and growly, singing, loud or quiet, different accents, getting louder from a whisper to a shout. If it is inconvenient to sit in a circle, number the students around the room and tell them to say their names in that order.

Concept

Getting to know you starters

Knowing a little more about other learners without being overly intrusive helps create a sense of trust and belonging among groups and it is easy for us to overlook the importance of social interaction in the learning process. Doing these games in a fun way helps later learning and is worth spending some time on. Activities that encourage the students to move around are also good icebreakers, because they usually end up standing next to someone they don't know. An activity in which students change places, for example if they agree with a statement, lead to mixing up the group, as do games like 'The Sun Shines On' (see p43) and 'Fruit Salad' (see p43). 'Find Someone Who' (see p47) takes up more time but students will find out a lot of information about each other which certainly helps to break the ice.

Application

Things in Common
Split the group into pairs. They have one minute to find five things they have in common. Now put two pairs together. They have a further minute to find three things they all have in common.

Twos and Threes
Divide the class into groups of five. In each group, in a limited time, students have to find out as many things as possible that three of them have in common but the other two don't. For example, three might have brown eyes and the other two green and blue; three might have brothers and the other two are only children or only have sisters.

Three Truths and a Lie
Everyone writes four pieces of information about themselves, three true one false, on a piece of paper. For example 'I love football', 'I'm a great dancer'. Everyone mingles and on the signal to stop pairs next to each other share their statements and try to guess which is the lie. On the signal start the process again.

Concept

Putting students into teams

Working in groups and teams can be lots of fun, but it's always worth spending some time considering how to group the students. 'Get into groups!' is fine for some activities but it will lead to teams that are largely same gender, same ethnic group and same ability range. Also, there's a tendency for friendship groups to go off task. Some students will be reluctant to work with people they don't know, but they will be acquiring the important skill of getting along with other people.

It is possible to plan the teams in advance, ensuring a range of ability, gender and ethnic groupings in each team. It's a good idea to use your knowledge of the class to avoid personality clashes. If you're trying to keep friends apart, make sure that this is true for all teams, so that the groupings are clearly fair to all. If you prefer to group the students randomly, you can use a game to do this. A game like 'The Sun Shines On' (see p43) or 'Fruit Salad' (see p43) mixes students up; you can then go round the circle and count them into fives (or however many you need in a team), or number – 1, 2, 3 ,4, 5…, 1, 2, 3, 4, 5… and send each number to a different place in the room.

Application

Line Ups

This game does not need as much space as those played in a circle, but, ideally, there should be enough space for all the students to stand in a straight line. However, it can be played with the students lining up around the walls of a room. Indicate where the line will start (this represents the lowest number or the letter 'A') and where it will end (this represents the highest number or the letter 'Z'). The group have to arrange themselves in order. This could be the order of their birthdays, house numbers, the number of letters in their names, the number of their post code or their names in alphabetical order. It could relate to subject content; for example, give each student a card with a Fibonacci number on it or a date in history. Allow a couple of minutes, then, when the line is complete, get them each to shout out their date of birth, house number, and so on, to check how well they achieved the task.

If you want to make the activity harder, make them line up in order without speaking or whispering. They can use any other method they wish, for example, writing in the air, holding up a number of fingers, pointing to a number in the room, writing it on paper.

To split them up into smaller groups for another activity, either count in fives (or however many each group needs) along the line (the groups will be mixed up, but will have something in common, for example, birthdays close together, similar house numbers) or number them 1, 2, 3, 4, 5…, 1, 2, 3, 4, 5… along the line, and tell each number to go to a different place in the room.

Objects

Get hold of a number of related objects, for example, four farmyard animal toys, four balls, and so on. Put them in a bag and tell each student to take one without looking. Those with related objects make up each team.

Concept

Team building activities

Being able to work together as a team is an important skill for life. We can't expect that students placed into random teams will immediately get on well together and accept the roles they allocate each other. Before they take on any major challenges, they need to go through some team building exercises, where they all focus on a common aim. Many games, particularly those that do not end up with an outright winner, such as 'Hoops' (see p31) and 'Cans' (see p31) are good for team building. Instead of playing them as a whole class, divide the students up to play in their own teams.

Quizzes between the teams are also good for giving each team a sense of having a common aim. To make sure the whole team collaborates on the answers, ask questions leading to a guess or estimate, such as 'How long is the River Nile?' or 'What is the longest word in the English language?'.

Encourage teams to establish their own identity by choosing a name, preferably something relating to the activity they are undertaking. They could also design a badge or a logo, and even make up a team song.

Application

Team Clap
With one person leading, the team must try to produce one synchronized clap. No words or counting in is allowed; everyone must watch the leader. Members of the team should take it in turns to lead.

Vroom
Moving around the circle, everyone says their name as fast as they can. They must go in order and each must have said their full name before the next speaks. This creates a 'vroom' sound. The team can time themselves, then try to beat their own time.

Clap Trap
This is the same as 'Vroom', but using a clap rather than names. To make it harder, the team can try it with their eyes shut.

I'm an Individual!
This reminds team members that they are still individuals, even if they have a common aim. Each student needs a piece of A4 paper. They close their eyes and follow these instructions, without asking questions: fold the paper in half, tear the bottom left corner, fold in half again, tear the top right corner, fold in half again and tear the bottom left corner. The students should open their eyes and compare each other's results within their teams.

Rope Stand Up
Create a circle of rope big enough for everyone in the team to sit around its edge on the floor. The challenge is for everyone to stand up while holding and lifting the rope, without putting their hands down on the floor.

Team Step Over
Everyone stands side by side behind a line, or length of tape or rope, and has to step over and land at *exactly* the same time. This sounds easy but requires a lot of co-operation and agreement to get it precisely right.

Concept

Team challenges

Once the students are sorted into teams and have established a group identity through games, they need to face a bigger challenge. This may be another, more demanding game, a sporting contest or an activity related to a subject, such as producing a newspaper, information booklet or presentation. Create time in the timetable so that students might face a series of challenges related to a theme; for example, they could imagine that they are the only survivors of a shipwreck and have to overcome difficulties such as transporting themselves and their equipment over a series of hazards or building shelters from minimal materials.

As well as encouraging the participants to work towards a common objective, the team building activities and games should have made the students aware of the particular strengths of individuals in the team. When the major challenges begin, allow the students time to analyse what is required in a challenge and make sure that they allocate roles, so that all team members play to their strengths. In a longer-term piece of work, lasting over several sessions, like producing a newspaper, make sure that each session begins with planning and allocation tasks and ends with a review. In this sort of challenge, the students should set their own criteria for success in each task and assess whether these have been achieved at the end.

In all challenges, encourage students to try out different approaches and methods, which might reflect the different learning styles within the team. Make sure that they learn from their mistakes and remind them of the saying:

> 'If you do what you've always done, you'll get what you've always got.'

TIP:
Raccoon Circles are a good source of games for a variety of uses and can be found for free at www.teamworkandteamplay.com. The tape for Raccoon Circles is available from www.profabrics.co.uk.

Application

Hoops
Participants stand in a circle. They have to be linked in some way; if they are reluctant to hold hands, they can hold wrists or sleeves. Ask two participants to break apart for a moment and link up again with their hands through a hoop. The object of the game is to get the hoop all around the circle, without anyone letting go of the person next to them; the participants have to struggle their way through by stepping through the hoop and shrugging it over their shoulders. After one hoop has started to go around in one direction, put in another hoop going the other way. One person will end up with both hoops, and the other participants should be encouraged to shout out suggestions as to how to deal with them. You can put in as many hoops as you think the group will cope with. You can also experiment with different sized hoops; small ones will favour smaller people, so if adults and children are taking part together, children will have the advantage.

Cans
You need clean, catering size open tins (make sure there are no rough or sharp edges) or small plastic buckets. Participants sit on chairs in a circle. The object of the game is to get the can around the circle, without it touching the ground, using only legs and feet – no elbows or hands are allowed. After the first can has started to move round, put in another can going in the opposite direction.

Drainpipes
Give each team two or more pieces of plastic drainpipes (all teams must have the same total length) and a tennis ball. They must transport the ball as far as possible, using only the drainpipes, and they must not cover the ends of the drainpipes in any way. If the ball touches the floor, they must go back to the beginning.

Crate Journey
Using three crates and two planks, the team must travel as far as possible without touching the ground. Mark out a start line and show distances along the 'course' using markers.

Concept

Team review

Working in teams is not always easy. There will always be people we don't get on with and it is also important to remember that teams don't have to agree, learning often comes from handling differences constructively. So to make teamwork more fun it is useful to review how teams have been working together and do that in a supportive manner so that people can improve but don't feel picked upon. One way to do this is to exchange 'appreciations' so that every member of the group has to give and receive at least one appreciation, which will be written, for example, something along the lines of 'I really like the way you stayed calm when we did that difficult challenge'. A good way of doing this is have some envelopes with the team members' names on the wall. The team members write each comment on a postcard and put it in the envelope of the person it is about. The comments should be anonymous. You can check envelopes to make sure everyone gets a positive comment, teachers can join in to hand out appreciations. The envelopes are handed out at the end of the day.

TIP:
There are many review activities looking at teamwork. Contact your local outdoor centre or adviser – they are excellent sources of active review techniques. Also try www.reviewing.com as a source of reviews and ideas.

Application

Values Cards

Have 20 to 30 large cards with feelings and values words written on them such as 'excited', 'happy', 'depressed', 'moody', 'caring', 'intolerant', 'belonging', 'excluded' and so on. Display the cards on the floor or wall. Below are a list of process questions as examples. Add or subtract from these depending on how you think the group will react to each other. Sometimes teams will take time to be comfortable with talking like this with each other but if you work through it the process can make learning together more fun.

Go through the following first as individuals then discuss as a team.

1. **Pick a card that:**
   - you need less of.
   - the group needs more/less of.
   - describes how the group handles problems.
   - describes the group's attitudes towards each other.
   - you would like to talk about.
   - is the most important to you.
   - is the most important to all people.

2. **Which word right now:**
   - brings you the most joy.
   - gives you the most trouble.
   - typifies how you interact with people.
   - guides your life.
   - describes your attitude towards the Earth.
   - describes the attitude towards your community.

Concept

Memory and mnemonics

Learning tasks and particularly revision can be a much more positive experience if students are taught to maximize their ability to remember. Your memory is central to processing, storing and recalling information and all learning depends on it. Memory content is changed as it is both retrieved and processed so our memory is not like a filing cabinet! When students say, 'I don't know how to revise', they often mean they they're not sure how to work so that they can remember things. Simple memory techniques are relatively easy to learn and can help to give students an immediate feeling of success and achievement, which can impact on their future success.

The brain disregards what it doesn't need. Apparently around 70 per cent of what you learn in a day is gone in 24 hours, unless you intend to remember it and practise it. To improve your memory you need to create associations between things.

There are three sorts of memory:

1. Immediate memory – this holds information for a few seconds or passes it on to your:

2. Short-term or working memory – this can hold about seven items at one time. If information is not rehearsed immediately, or seen in your head, it will be forgotten in 30 seconds. It sifts, rejects or selects information to go into the:

3. Long-term memory – this holds millions of pieces of data. You have several long-term memories – including a visual memory, an auditory memory and a motor memory.

There are many active ways of encouraging memory to strengthen learning of a subject or topic. We start with ideas about memory, then look at review techniques to embed learning, some thinking skills ideas and starter suggestions to help build the linking of concepts and orientation towards a topic that is essential to get learning to 'stick' even better.

Application

Mnemonics

Mnemonics are simple aids to memory. They usually relate a sentence to the initial letters of words that have to be remembered in a particular order. If the sentence is absurd or funny, the brain is more likely to remember it. Mnemonics can be used in starter or review activities to help students to go over their learning in order to make it stick.

- May I have a large container of coffee? *Counting the letters of each word gives you the value of pi to seven places.*

- Kids Prefer Cheese Over Fried Green Spinach. *Kingdom, Phylum, Class, Order, Family, Genus, Species*

- Big Elephants Can Always Understand Small Elephants *Spelling of BECAUSE*

- Rhythm Helps Your Two Hips Move *Spelling of RHYTHM*

- Cows Often Sit Down Carefully. Perhaps Their Joints Creak? Persistent Early Oiling Might Prevent Painful Rheumatism. Order of geological time periods (*Cambrian, Ordovician, Silurian, Devonian, Carboniferous, Permian, Triassic, Jurassic, Cretaceous, Palaeocene, Eocene, Oligocene, Miocene, Pliocene, Pleistocene, Recent*)

- 'My very educated mother just served us nine pizzas' *The planets in order.*

Perhaps the best mnemonics, however, are those that students make up themselves, using associations that mean something to them. Setting students the task of making up mnemonics for topics just studied is a useful review activity.

Concept

More memory fun

We tend to forget if we:

- don't understand
- don't take in information in the first place
- are distracted
- don't feel good
- are confused
- don't want to remember
- don't rehearse and practise things
- don't think it's important enough
- are anxious about trying to remember things.

Some things are easy to remember, such as what we do every day, places or songs we know well, what has happened recently, occasions that stick out because they are special, like holidays and birthdays, or times when we have been very happy or very sad.

Our short-term memories are generally only capable of holding about seven items at once, but there are techniques we can use to improve this. There are lots of fun ways to remember things and most memory activities are more likely to stick if they are active. Association, or linking, is one of the ways our memory holds on to information. We need to be able to link things to each other in order to remember them more easily. Categorizing – making associations between things – also helps us to remember. We remember the categories, then we recall the items in each.

It's a good idea to do a memory test first, then to try out some concepts that involve linking and chunking up ideas that need to be learned. Students will remember the memory concepts themselves and use them more readily if they've had a chance to have a go at them in a fun way.

Application

Here are some concepts for remembering.

The Tray Game (Kim's game)

1. Gather together 15–20 everyday objects. Try to ensure that they don't all fall into obvious categories.

2. Place them on a tray and cover with a cloth. Make sure that all the students in the group can see the objects.

3. Uncover the tray. Allow the students one minute to study the objects, then cover them again.

4. Ask for a couple of volunteers to try to remember as many objects as they can.

5. Ask all the students to write down or sketch as many objects as they can.

6. It's unlikely that many students will remember more than ten objects. Go on to the activities below to try out some ways of remembering.

Making Associations

Place three of the objects in front of the group and ask them to find a way of linking them, for example, they are all the same colour, they all begin with the same letter, they are all manufactured, they all have straight edges. Don't try to find things that have obvious links; the students should work hard on trying to connect them. Some might relate them to their own lives, or make up a story.

Chunking

Ask the students to look at the tray and see if they fit into different categories. This might be colours, first letters or shapes. Some of the objects might be stationery, some might be clothing, some might relate to food. Remind the students that short-term memory finds it hard to hold more than about seven items at one time, so it is easier to remember all the objects category by category.

Finally, play the Tray Game again with different objects so that the students can try out their new skills.

Visualization: 'a picture speaks a thousand words'

The underlying principles of an excellent memory are *imagination* and *association*. Using your mind's eye to create pictures can have a profound effect on your ability to recall information. This process of creating images in your head is called visualization. But visualization involves more than seeing only pictures in your mind. You should be able to imagine sounds, textures, tastes and smells. The fun thing about using your imagination is that anything can happen, which allows you to use exaggeration and humour, both of which make the experience more memorable. Research has shown that using positive and pleasant images for visualization is more effective because the brain may be reluctant to return to negative images.

The better you can visualize, the more powerful your memory will become. Visualization can be used in a variety of ways in learning; to stimulate and anchor the learning when it first takes place and as a tool for recall.

Application

To **work the imagination**, ask the students to find a space in the room where they can sit comfortably in a small place of their own. Tell them that in a moment you will be asking them to close their eyes. Try playing some baroque music quietly in the background.

Now ask the students to create a mental picture of the following things with their eyes closed. Encourage them to create as realistic a picture as possible, using all their senses all the time they are given to build up the image. Some of the images are, initially, harder that others. It is important to give students time to settle into each separate scene. You may want to prompt them by asking them a few questions, for example, What can you see? Look in detail at colour, form, texture.

How do you feel? How does your body feel? Be aware of all your different senses.

1. Yourself sitting in the room where you sleep.

2. Your school bag on a table.

3. The taste of freshly cut lemon.

4. Your hand being plunged into ice-cold water.

5. Being hit with a feather pillow.

6. Putting your hand in some soil in the garden.

7. The taste of lemonade.

8. An empty classroom.

9. The taste of chocolate ice-cream.

10. Stepping out of a warm house into the street in the middle of winter.

Notice their reactions as they visualize. For example, many often grimace when re-creating the lemon taste (even though there is nothing physically there!). Some people claim that they actually 'tasted' the lemonade – that's the power of the imagination.

Gather the students' reactions to this activity. How easy or difficult did they find it? How powerful do they think their imagination is? How can their imagination be useful in learning/revision?

Concept

Visualization: association

The ability to use your imagination and visualize is something that gets better with practice, although some people do find it easier than others.

Linking what needs to be remembered to something that is stable and constant in the mind is establishing association. Therefore, linking new learning to old can speed up recall. Using a narrative to help linking that builds upon something that is so familiar to you helps to add the further dimension of sequence and order. You might think that holding all those images in your memory might overload it, but in fact, if you build a story of the right length research suggests that it helps to anchor learning in long-term memory. Again, it is a matter of practice and trying visualizations that are personal and meaningful to each individual.

Application

This is another technique for visualization and can help with exam revision. Ask students to list about a dozen keywords or concepts from a topic that you are revising (or give them a list). Again, you need to ask the students to sit quietly and close their eyes and build up a picture in their minds as you rehearse a script.

Imagine yourself standing outside a front door. Try to visualize it as vividly as possible, noting the colour of the paint, the position of the doorbell and so on. Place the first concept in front of the door. The only problem is that you might not see such a small object on the floor. So, solve that problem by imagining it as huge, so big that you have to climb over it to get to the front door.

Ask students to visualize a walk through their house and place an item in a room or on a piece of furniture. At the end of the list ask students to write their list from memory re-creating the route they took.

Reassure students that they will get better the more they use the technique. They can try testing themselves at the end of the day, week and month! How can this technique help us with revision? What kind of things might we try to visualize?

Concept

Active review: physical games

Physical games are fun and they have a number of uses in learning:

- As icebreakers and warm ups.
- For team building.
- To provide a break between one part of a lesson and another.
- To give students (and teachers) an opportunity for some movement after a long period of deskbound work.
- As a reward for hard work and participation.

However, they can also be related to review and thinking:

- To reinforce learning in a kinesthetic and active way.
- To allow some time for learning to be unconsciously processed.
- To use language in an active way.
- To test recall through quick decision making.

If you're planning games, you obviously need to take some practicalities into consideration. Though there are a large number of games that can be played in the classroom, some of them need a lot of space. Circle games need enough room for all the students to arrange their chairs into a circle. There are health and safety considerations, too. Games that require changing places are probably safer on a non-slip surface like a carpet. Always establish ground rules, positively worded if possible, with the students before you start – for example, 'walking only' and be consistent in applying them, preferably with young people self-monitoring.

Application

Active review: circle games

The Sun Shines On

Participants sit on chairs in a circle, with one person standing in the centre. There must be a chair for every participant apart from the person standing. The person in the centre shouts, 'The Sun shines on…' for example '…everyone wearing black shoes', '…everyone with brown eyes', '…everyone who owns a pet'. Anyone who this applies to must stand up and swap seats. The person in the centre must try to get to a chair. The person left standing in the middle then continues by shouting, 'The Sun shines on…' and so on.

Subject application: This game can provide a 'safe' way for students to express their views. Give some of the students specific statements to make in the centre, for example, 'The Sun shines on everyone who thinks a good attitude is important for learning', '…everyone who thinks Henry V was a good king', '…everyone who had difficulty doing their homework last night'.

Fruit Salad

Participants sit on chairs in a circle, with one person standing in the middle. Go round the circle, giving everybody the name of a fruit (four fruits in all) for example, apple, orange, grape and plum (the person in the middle needs a fruit as well). The person in the middle shouts out the name of the fruits in any combination, for example, 'apple', 'grape and plum'. They can call 'fruit salad' which means that everybody must move. Whichever 'fruits' are called must stand up and change places; the person in the middle must try to get a seat. The person left in the middle becomes the next caller.

Subject application: Students could be given the names of characters or objects which group together in some way, for example, for *Romeo and Juliet* each student could have the name of a different character, as far as possible. The caller can then call out 'Capulets', 'Montagues', 'Neither side', or, more subtly, 'Romeo's friends', 'Capulets' servants', and so on.

Application

Active review:
True/False Run Around

A True/False review is an active way of checking out what young people remember from previous lessons or finding out what they already know about a topic that is coming up. All you need is a set of true/false questions on any subject. Run around is an active and fun way of using them but it is essential to have enough space for young people to move around safely.

This is a very active way of using the True/False concept. It might be necessary to rearrange the classroom to allow children to move around without bumping into each other. Designate one wall as TRUE and the other as FALSE by sticking up posters. The children stand in the middle. When each statement is read, shout, 'Run around!' and the children move towards the wall they consider to be correct. Put a time limit on this, by counting down or playing music, so that they stand still wherever they are when the countdown ends or the music stops.

A more sedate way of using True/False is to give each person a card with TRUE on one side and FALSE on the other (or they could write them on their individual whiteboards). They then hold up the side that they think is correct.

Alternatively, young people can work in groups, each group deciding together whether they think each statement is true or false. To make this competitive, groups may be given points for each correct answer.

Application

Active review: memory map

This technique is taken from the Northumberland Thinking Skills series and is really good fun to put in as a group problem-solving and memory game that can reinforce a subject area. Students work in groups and have to reproduce a map that is at the front of the class on a piece of paper at their desks. The groups get two minutes or so to decide their strategy, then are allowed to send one person at a time to come up to the front and look at the map, but only for 10 seconds. They then return and reproduce as much of it as possible. Carry on until each person has had at least two turns and then compare results with the original. Using maps helps to reinforce work on map symbols and grids for example, but pictures of say an historic building can be used.

Colour
Pictures
Words
+ Fun
_____
= Memorable mind maps!

Concept

Find someone who

Sometimes called a People Scavenger Hunt, or Human Bingo, Find Someone Who... sets each group member the task of collecting other members of the group who have particular knowledge, skills or expertise. This activity encourages students to ask each other questions and to look upon other people as a source of information. This activity is useful as an icebreaker, group co-operation and review exercise.

The students should be encouraged to approach as many of their classmates as possible, particularly if this is an activity to encourage them to mix, by only allowing them to write down any name once. Students find this activity fun when teachers and other adults join in, though you might not want to do that if you are trying to find out how much they know! You can set a time limit and see who has collected the most names at the end, or go on until one participant has collected a name for every question. It is a good idea to have a signal to show that someone has finished, for example, ringing a bell.

Application

Make a list of statements – about 12 to 15 are a good number for a class of 30.

Each student will need their own sheet with the questions and a space next to each to write down the name of the person they have found who can answer it. Students go round questioning each other until they find someone who can answer the statement, when they write down the name. At the end of the search, go through at least one completed sheet and ask the students named to talk about some of the statements they matched. It is also a good idea to talk about any statements that students could not match.

So, for example, if there had been a topic on the solar system questions might include:

Find someone who knows the answers to these questions...

   ...Which planet is closest to the Sun?

   ...Which planet is called the Red Planet?

   ...Can you name one of Jupiter's moons?

   ...Which is the smallest planet?

   ...Which planet has rings?

The children do not write down the answers to the questions but the names of their classmates who can answer them. This activity can be used as an icebreaker by using more personal and humorous questions (for example, draw a cartoon, roll their tongues and so on.)

Concept

How many ways to review?

Constant review and feedback are essential to help students make sense of the meanings for themselves. Reviews do not always have to take long, in fact little and often can be a very good policy. Making reviews fun and active helps the learning process. Asking people 'what have they learned' is too open and floors most learners, so using different review processes helps to organize and structure thinking while the novelty engages the important intuitive side of thinking. Earlier in this section we looked at some active reviews. The ideas opposite are fun to do and involve little moving around. How many different ways as a teacher can you compile and do you share them frequently with your colleagues? If not, why not?!

Application

Forbidden Words
Give one student a card with the title of a topic that they are going to talk about and five related words that they must not use. For example, in a citizenship session about crime, the topic might be 'Trial' and the forbidden words would be 'judge', 'court', 'sentence', 'jury' and 'defendant'. While the student talks about the subject, others in the group have to guess what the topic is. Whoever guesses correctly becomes the next person to talk on a topic.

A–Z Review
Students can work in pairs or trios. On an A4 sheet of paper have the alphabet A–Z written out in sequence; against each letter of the alphabet students have to write a word from the lesson that begins with that letter. Some imagination for x, y and z is allowed! To energize this activity only 2, 3 or 5 minutes is allowed.

Odd One Out
Students work in small groups. Write a series of trios of words from the topic or subject that has been worked on; groups have to use their knowledge of their work to say which is the odd one out. Feed back as a class to say why they made the choice. Some trios may have only one answer, some may be deliberately ambiguous.

Traffic Lights
Students have a set of red, orange and green 'lollipop' cards. As a class talk through the lesson together from the beginning, recalling it in sequence. At each point where a key concept or idea was raised students raise a coloured lollipop depending on their level of understanding. So for example raise red if not understood, green if understood and amber if not sure and would like some more explanation.

Concept

Dramatic review

Not everyone likes drama, song or dance but many do, and if you work in a supportive group everyone can participate. With this concept the idea is to re-create a piece of learning in a short performance that can be a play, mime, tableau, poem, rap or song. Give some advance warning of the challenge and allow some time for groups to prepare their chosen piece. Create a supportive atmosphere of celebration and fun and have each group perform in turn. Groups can create their own names and these can be drawn out of a hat to establish a running order.

The fun of creating the piece not only aids processing of information but in the act of performing, students have to have understood the learning in order to re-create in another symbolic form.

Application

Advertising review

Divide the groups into teams (see p26) and ask each team to think of a name for themselves. The teams are given some time to re-create a well-known advert but using the themes of the learning topic. Encourage an atmosphere of celebration and support and have each team perform in turn.

A collection of adverts and jingles can be gathered together as models if teams are unsure about which ones to use.

Concept

Drama in learning

Watching good drama teachers in action is a real privilege and they have many skills that can help bring concepts alive in an active and fun way. There are many books on drama, and some research is needed if you are to get the best out of them, but in a secondary school the drama department should be a real source of fun thinking activities that you could adapt. Drama activities can involve a lot of team and language work and the opportunity to get up and move about – so they should appeal to a range of students.

Drama in education is a creative vehicle for teaching across the curriculum and a dynamic means of engaging students with the world around them. Through drama learners can seek empathy for others and make meanings more personal to themselves. There are many drama techniques most of us could use quite quickly. Hot Seating (p53) is one that most teachers should be comfortable with and can be adapted to a number of subject areas. Again, like a lot of activities, if it is used too frequently it can become very dull.

> **TIP:**
> See *With Drama in Mind: real learning in imagined worlds* by Patrice Baldwin for a good overview in this area (p96). Look particularly at the summary of the 'Mantle of Expert' concept (from Dorothy Heathcote) – potentially very powerful. And talk to your nearest drama department!

Application

In this activity the teacher goes into role and takes on the persona of someone to be interviewed, and the class become journalists seeking information for their paper or documentary programme. So, for example, in history you could be the survivor from a famous battle, or a politician about to put a bill through Parliament, or you could be a famous artist or a well-known scientist. The possibilities are endless. Divide the class into teams and give each team time to prepare a set of questions to elicit information from the character. Talk about how the teams will each have to produce their own paper front page, or news script, complete with headlines, so discuss and model what might be good questions (open ones) or poor questions for getting a story out of the character.

Having allowed what you feel is a reasonable time for getting a set of questions, then take the hot seat as your character as in a 'press conference'. Don't put on accents or mannerisms. This exercise is about thinking yourself into the role so that you can provide information for the journalists. You might want to use some of the personality of the character but it doesn't need an accent. You will need to have researched the character, or have a potted biography to hand, or have information that allows you to make some reasonable assumptions. The idea is to reply from the point of view of the character and provide a different viewpoint to the one young people may already have. This is about gently disturbing their thinking as well as information gathering. Teams can take turns to ask questions, and allow what you feel is an appropriate time. After the press conference teams can produce their front pages for display.

Concept

Quickfire creatives

Creativity is a much used and often misunderstood word, and as a process often involves a lot of very hard slog. However, the process should be imbued with many moments of fun and laughter. One of the elements of creative thinking is building up good habits. Playing games that build up language skills can be one of the ways of developing these habits.

Creativity can be modelled in many ways, for example discussing who are creative people and what creative ideas are. Find out about how these people worked and how the ideas came about; for instance, a famous car advert that has parts creatively knocking into each other took months and months of exhausting retakes to make. The inventor of Velcro had been looking for a quick fastener for years and had given up until he walked through a field and a burr stuck to his leg.

We need to use a variety of tools at our disposal: quick thinking, slow thinking, intuition, hunches and taking risks.

Application

'I am the Sun'

This can be played in a circle or with people standing at the front. Space is needed for people to move easily. Someone stands up and says 'I am the Sun'; anyone who can make a connection comes out to join them saying what the link is. For example 'I am the Moon'. Another person comes out with a link, for example 'I am a newspaper'. The first person (the Sun) then chooses one of the links to stay at the front (for example, the Moon) and the 'Sun' and the non-chosen sit down. The person remaining states their link again, for example 'I am the Moon' and the process is repeated. The game is a good energizer to build up quickfire links and associations. You could start with a keyword from a topic and encourage students to make quickfire links.

1001 Uses

Gather together a group of 6–8 everyday items. Divide students into teams and ask them to brainstorm as many uses for the items as they can think of. The idea is to encourage as many unusual and lateral uses as possible; it doesn't matter how ridiculous they might seem. Often creative ideas emerge from letting our imaginations run wild.

Another variation on this is to put a cylinder on the table such as the cardboard tube from a kitchen paper roll. Tell students that this cylinder might fall over soon and ask them to brainstorm as many ideas as quickly as they can as to why the tube might fall over by itself.

These activities work well if given a finite time and a sense of urgency is encouraged.

Concept

It's a mystery!

One of the key concepts in learning is being able to ask the right questions and that is not always an easy thing to do. So we need some intriguing ways of modelling the process. The Northumberland Thinking Skills Project uses the concept of mysteries as a way of engaging learners not only in questioning skills but pulling thinking together around the subject. The mystery has a central question and clues are presented that might help students to solve the questions. The clues could be objects such as artefacts or clothes, or written on cards. This concept is particularly useful in humanities where there is a strong narrative thread about people to whom things happen. It is important to base the mystery around real events and real people and personalizing it through a local connection makes it all the more powerful.

This concept is a fun way of engaging a range of thinking skills such as sorting, inference, synthesizing and speculating, as it allows learners to literally 'handle' the ideas and move them around physically while talking about them. It should be used in the context of a raft of other linking activities for the subject.

> **TIP:**
> See *Thinking Through Geography* and *Thinking Through History* (p96) for lesson ideas that are easily adapted.

Application

A Mystery Example

Take the story of a group of people or an individual from a history topic being studied and find an intriguing question. For example from World War I ask 'Why Did Tom Go To War?'. Tom is a fictional character that combines elements of what we know about young men going to the front at that time. Put the question on an envelope, inside which are 15–30 cards that give a sentence of information that might help students answer the question. Some information might give personal details (for example age, social background, employment), details about place and time, background factors (for example employment patterns, local recruiting patterns, family feelings about the war), 'trigger factors' (for example recruitment policy, local regiment, family connections) and throw in a few red herrings as well.

In groups, the students have to sift through the information to answer the question. So they could start by sorting into 'reasons to join the army' and 'other information'. They could then prioritize the information in order of importance.

It is very important to have a class debrief and get learners to justify why they chose that order and what the evidence is suggesting.

Concept

Visual mapping

There are many forms of visual mapping that can help learners to sort and abstract information, link ideas, plan and organize learning, and literally put our thoughts on the table. This helps to make learning more fun when students can almost 'see' what is inside their heads and have a tool that makes organizing easier. Mind Mapping® has become a well-known and popular thinking tool, but while this process can help many learners not everyone can use mind maps easily. It is worth taking time to find a variety of visual tools that can be used by students for different purposes. Their novelty is often fun but when they are used as part of regular learning habits, students can be highly motivated by finding a visual that really suits their thinking in that subject. Some of them make excellent planning tools for teachers as well.

TIP:
For a range of visual tools, look at *Thinking Skills and Eye Q: visual tools for raising intelligence* (see p96).

Application

This is a commonly used visual tool to help demonstrate the structure of a topic or concept. The idea is to reveal all the relationships in the overall concept and how its constituent parts may be organized. Concept maps can be used to explore understanding in a topic or as a demonstration of what students have understood. It is often better to start with a completed one and model the process for learners.

Working in small groups and using post-it notes that can be placed on a desk or wall, students write each element of a topic on a separate note. They are then arranged and grouped into categories of words that might go together. Then for each group or category see if the notes can be arranged into some hierarchy of importance. When groups are happy with their arrangement, tidy it up by sticking the notes onto a piece of flip chart paper and draw lines between the words to show relationships. Write on the lines to describe relationships. Each group feed back and discuss decisions.

Variation: Another way of doing this is for the teacher to have pre-prepared words on cards or for groups to do words to give to other teams.

There may more than one way of mapping a topic and this produces a good discussion.

Concept

Physical models

We often see learners grasp ideas and concepts once they have been able to physically map it or model it out. For example we use number lines and real objects to grasp the importance of place and value in our abstract symbols of mathematics. Some learners who are struggling with sentence construction in their writing are encouraged when they can 'walk' out a sentence while talking it through. Unless they hear and visualize the process it is very difficult for some students to translate into a symbolic form. A person who is into dance or martial arts can talk through an idea while constructing the movement and then sort their thinking while mentally rehearsing that movement. We need as many tools and props as we can find so that the learner can make sense of the process for themselves.

We believe that one of the reasons for this is that the motor systems in our brain are also those used to form metaphorical concepts, and metaphor is the basis of our thinking: for example, think of the metaphors you might use to describe your feelings such as low, high, exciting and depressing and they will more likely relate to a physical space, level or a metaphor of movement. More time is often needed than we allow learners for physically 'playing' with knowledge.

Building a model that relies on either a literal or metaphorical understanding of a topic helps to consolidate the underlying concepts. This model does not always have to use materials. For example, you could have fun reproducing the digestive tract or the water cycle using the students themselves to be in the right places and label their part. Ask them to do a mime for their piece of the jigsaw. Then put the mimes together in the right sequence, or enact the journey of a water droplet or food particle.

Application

The 3D Model

For this application get students into teams of 4–5 at most. Gather together paperclips, tubes from kitchen rolls, newspaper, glue and sticky tape and give the same items to each group. Ask the students to build a 3D model to represent the concept or topic they have been learning. This will be a metaphor for the subject and the better they have grasped the topic the more imaginative the models will be. It helps the design process to set it in a framework. First explain the challenge, tell them they have ten minutes to plan their structure – they mustn't start, then ten minutes to construct, then each class walks round to see the models with each group talking through their structures as the class arrives at it. The time limits are strictly observed so as to build team-thinking skills and engage students through framing it as a challenge.

The more creative and imaginative groups will have reflected a greater grasp of the topic they have modelled

Concept

'Doodle' fun

This concept has a similar rationale to that on p60 as it is another way of representing knowledge, thinking visually and then talking it through. Thinking is a complex and highly nuanced process, and remember that it is we who like to categorize it and make up skills taxonomies. Just because we come up with a list of thinking skills does not mean we work like that.

There are some eminent scientists who argue that we are just part of the creative processes in the universe and that we should look at the unity in life forces. Whether we agree or not, the point is finding an individual learning journey that makes sense for us.

Constructing and drawing our own maps or symbols or cartoons can be a valid and fun way of deepening our understanding, because as we represent something graphically we have to translate the learning into our own words. To check that this is not an aimless exercise for students, they also have to talk through their drawings and explain the symbolic meaning.

Application

This application has a similar rationale to the 3D challenge on p61 but involves only marker pens and flip chart paper. The groups have to come up with a number of symbols or doodles that represent their understanding. Not as easy as it sounds, but some students are really engaged by mark making and abstract marks can be turned into powerful thinking ideas.

For example a spiral doodle might symbolize a journey through the concept with different symbols in the spiral to represent each component. You need to play with this one and model it. Display the symbols on the wall for people to explain, leave them up for a while then revisit them and see if they still carry the same meaning.

Ask students to keep all their doodles as they go along and make them into a graphic story of their learning journey.

Concept

Some starter fun

Starters help students connect to their previous learning, but this might not always be about content. Some starters help students think about themselves as learners and what they need to achieve. At the start of the lesson, ask students to assess their progress and achievements in previous lessons. As soon as they know the focus for this session, they should set targets for themselves or consider what they want to get out of it. Students in pairs can recap what they covered in the previous sessions and decide together what they think will be important about this one.

Starters can also encourage students to practise some of the techniques they will use in the session, such as sequencing or predicting. Devising questions on the topic of the lesson is a way of thinking around it and looking at it from a number of angles.

There are a number of starters you can make into game or puzzle-like activities. Fun starters help orient learners to concepts and connect to what they might already know. Frequent starter and reviewing techniques become part of a circle of learning that helps students embed memory and have fun applying what they know.

Application

Timeline

Give out statements about work relating to the topic of the lesson, including previous and future learning on the topic, one statement per student or pair. Tell the students to arrange themselves into a single line, with each statement in order.

Questions

Give each student or pair five minutes to make up as many questions on a topic as they can think of. Compile a list of questions from the whole class and, as a class, try to answer them or work out how to find out the answers.

Predictions

Tell the students the topic of the lesson and ask them to make predictions as to what the session will contain.

Letters

Give each student a letter of the alphabet and tell him or her to think of one or more words connected to the topic of today's lesson that begin with that letter.

Keywords

Give each student a card with a keyword from the topic they are studying and tell them to find the student with the keyword most closely related to theirs. Pairs should then find other pairs whose words connect to theirs. If there is enough space, all the students can arrange their cards on the floor, showing the connections between the keywords.

Poster Match

Give out various pictures or cartoons relating to the forthcoming topic and ask students to match with other people's that might be closely related, and explain why. For example different landscape features could be related to a topic on erosion. There could be more than one right answer.

Make Some More

To get students used to a long and complicated word that is going to arise, ask them to make as many words out of it as they can in the first five minutes.

Concept

Spelling fun!

Can learning spelling be fun? For some students it comes naturally, others enjoy playing with words and spellings but many of us struggle to learn to spell. There are many strategies you can use to practise and remember spellings. Each student will have a different way of remembering. Mnemonics are helpful, or using a dance or movement routine as you say the spelling, or using lots of colours in big posters: there are as many ways as people have imagination to find.

Just sticking to one method, say a phonic rule, may not be helpful for some. The fun is in discovering imaginative ways that help you remember the rule. There are a few to consider on the opposite page.

> **TIP:**
> Use spellings as a research activity with students, either getting them to write down their tricky words or giving them lists of difficult words, and then providing them with a range of strategies to use: for example, movement, rote learn, colour, sound, pair and share, and so on. Which strategy works best for them? Do they work every time?

Application

These are a few ideas that involve movement and can be done with other people, either at home or in groups, so that you can support each other to get it right.

- Go for a walk or make up a dance routine as you say the spellings out loud.

- Write out the letters of each spelling on pieces of card, shuffle them up and put them back in order.

- Using post-it notes, write down each of the spellings. Assemble the notes on the wall, grouping any similar patterns together. How many different ways of grouping the words can you find?

- With your group spell out a word, using your bodies or any other resources provided to make the letters.

- Spell out the word, writing it in the air with your hand. As you do this, say the letters out loud.

- Count the number of letters in each word. Then hold up that number of fingers as you spell the word. This will help you check you have included the right number of letters in the spelling.

- Working in pairs, take it in turns to write the spellings of the word on your partner's back. Your partner has to guess what word you have written.

Concept

Big number fun

Numbers can fascinate some learners and leave others cold. Sometimes we can have fun doing some odd and playful investigations into number and gain a sense of how the units they describe relate to each other, and how large numbers might relate to describing the real world.

The applications here could be a fun way of playing with number so as to develop estimation skills and hunches about what numbers can do for us.

Application

Present some challenges in a playful manner that require some computation and connection to other pieces of learning. For example:

'What happened 1,000,000,000 seconds ago in this country?'

'How long is your digestive tract?'

'If I walked overland to Beijing how many strides would it take?'

'If I walked through the Earth to get to China how many strides, and could I do it in theory?'

'If I laid 100,000 one pence pieces out in a straight line where would they end up?'

Discuss what kind of information is needed to complete these challenges and the thinking strategies that might be employed. Feed back how you found out.

Concept

Exam fun?!

Believe it or not, a few people enjoy exams but we won't pretend there are many of them! Exams are things we have to do and they can be a slog, but that doesn't mean to say that we can't have some fun trying to coach students to become more successful at them. Having a positive belief is important and there are techniques to help that in this book.

We learn unconsciously as well as consciously. So when getting ready for exams, posters, post-it notes, mind maps and so on, displayed everywhere possible means that students are learning even when they think they are not. We love colour! It's easily memorable and is a great organizational tool for revision. Students should be encouraged to flood their environment with visual material, to use highlighter pens and to try their hand at drawing cartoons, pictures, mind maps and so on. One of the key things we can do is coach students with the kind of language exams use and give them opportunities to understand the terms.

Application

Use a space that people can move around in. Prepare sets of cards with typical exam terms on, for example, contrast, explain, outline.

Prepare sets with matching definitions on. Have equal numbers of each and enough for each student.

Give all the cards out at random then ask students to circulate in order to match the correct term to its definition. Repeat the process so students become familiar with a wide range of terms.

Group Exam Tip

Divide the students into groups of four or five. Give each group some Monopoly or pretend money to the value of £100 made up of 3 x £20, 3 x £10, 2 x £5. Give each group an envelope with 20 exam tips written on cards, for example, 'get a good night's sleep' or 'if you are running out of time use notes to complete the answer'.

The group have to decide on eight tips to spend the money on and decide how much the tips they have chosen are worth. They then feed back to the whole class on why they spent the money the way that they did.

Ask each student which tip is worth £50 to them and ask them to explain why to the other students.

Concept

Self-relaxation

There are many relaxation techniques that can be used quickly and simply and can help learners in moments of stress not to feel overwhelmed and to avoid panic. They can also help learners to prepare themselves for a difficult process.

In exams, when the mind suddenly goes blank, it is worth coaching students into doing a little self-relaxation exercise to help them anchor their thoughts again.

TIP:
There is a script for a visualization exercise on p217 of *Brian Friendly Revision* (see p96).

Application

There are a number of visualization exercises that can be done to help students relieve stress when approaching or even during exams. One simple way is to close your eyes and work from head to toe visualizing each body part floating and relaxing as you picture it; imagine the feeling of lightness in each part until the body feels as if it is floating.

Reverse the process working from toe to head, lightly grounding the body into a safe and relaxing environment where you feel safe.

Try visualizing!

Concept

Humour

Something is more likely to stick in the brain if we find it funny, which is why your class forget their seven-times table but always remember the time when your chair collapsed while you were sitting on it!

Humour can help to create a relaxed atmosphere and defuse a difficult one. Jokes and puns can encourage students to think about language and to remember vocabulary and terminology.

There are now special laughter clubs all over the world; they began in India. Not everyone shares the same sense of humour but jokes and funny stories, if used with care and sensitivity, make good sources of cross-cultural understanding. Although an obvious point to make, remember that we laugh with rather than at.

Application

Jokes

A child comes home from his first day at school. His mother asks: 'What did you learn today?'

The child replies: 'Not enough. I have to go back tomorrow.'

Like anything if done to death, jokes can become extremely irritating; however, having a reputation as a teller of terrible (but non-offensive) jokes can stand a teacher in good stead. A daily pun is certain to raise a groan or two! You could make up your own jokes, or you could collect them; the internet is a very plentiful source. Making jokes does not come easily to some but having a fund of them helps to model the structures that are used. Can you start every day with a new joke and encourage students to find one to match? Also, funny poetry (see Roger McGough, for instance) can be enjoyed by people of all ages. Exploring humour and playing with words in the way poetry does is a good way of encouraging a rich appreciation of how language works.

Also note that humour as an issue can raise serious discussion about what is offensive or acceptable to different people, and these discussions should not be avoided as they are of real interest to young people. A citizenship lesson could be an ideal place to discuss some of the serious issues jokes can raise about, for example, gender and culture.

If you want a fun way of putting students into pairs for work, make enough cards for each young person, write a different punchline on half the cards and the joke starters on the other half. Give the cards out at random and ask students to match punchline to starter.

Concept

The physical learning environment

There are many factors in the learning environment that can contribute to the fun of learning: colour, visuals, music, natural light (some research suggests that daylight bulbs are far better than some of the old neon ones), temperature, smell and air quality all help comfort and sensory stimulation. Of course, few teachers have complete control over the spaces they have to work in, but it may be possible to improve some elements of the environment, if not all.

Obviously the outdoor environment, which includes a good use of the school grounds, and visits are huge sources of fun learning opportunities and should be planned carefully with all the risks in mind. There are many 'treasures' on our doorsteps that with a little imagination can be turned into fascinating objects to be 'hunted' to enrich learning. Visitors to the classroom add another essential element of difference and motivation to the learning environment.

Application

The Wool Wide Web

Life is connected in so many ways, and much of our learning is about making connections between concepts, facts and abstract ideas. If the space in a classroom restricts the use of physically modelling ideas, then think about how the walls and windows can display interesting and colourful posters, pictures and topic ideas from different subjects.

Every so often a group of students can be asked to pin coloured wool between pictures and ideas on display that may be linked in some way. At a different time another group with another colour can be asked to find different connections. A poster can have more than one connection. A web should appear with nodes and clusters. Discuss why they chose the connections and what the patterns are telling us.

Be imaginative about finding good material from a range of areas that contribute to a topic, for example what links around global warming and climate change can be made between pictures of the water cycle, climate models, history of the Industrial Revolution, agricultural production, transport and mathematics, and so on.

Concept

Using music

Music adds a sensory dimension to any learning space. It can help reduce stress and anxiety, particularly as students enter the room, perhaps apprehensive about the lesson that's coming up. It can support periods of quiet reflection and stimulate creativity. Music can help to counteract the effects of a cold and empty environment. It can also raise energy levels and produce a state of relaxed awareness which is ideal for receptive learning.

In recent years, some research has led to a belief that baroque music – that written between about 1600 and 1750 – is the most effective for learning, possibly because it has 60 beats per minute, which is very much like the beating of your heart when it is relaxed. However, many students will be resistant to Mozart and Bach because it's 'classical' music; try to find something more modern with the same rhythmic pattern. It does appear that instrumental music is the best for learning, because it is easy to be distracted by words.

Experiment with different types of music to find the best to suit your purpose. For example, to energize you need something upbeat, whereas for relaxation something slower would be better. Make sure you use a variety of music and don't have it on all the time, so that you and the students forget it's there. If some of them remain hostile to the type of music you choose, have a session occasionally where you allow them to bring in music they like and discuss what appeals to them about it.

Application

Some suggested uses of music in the classroom:

■ To create the right atmosphere at the beginning of a session, theme or process. This can help to anchor the learning by providing a memorable association.

■ To close a session, theme or process.

■ To enliven breaks with background music.

■ To encourage relaxation and reduce stress.

■ To change the energy levels of a group – this can be to calm down a group that's too lively or to energize a group that is too quiet.

■ As an aid to visualization.

■ To provide a soundtrack to role plays or presentations.

■ As a stimulus for creative activities like writing or painting.

■ To create an association, which can be used later to recall the learning.

Concept

The enquiry environment

A lot of the activities in this section are about creating an environment of puzzlement and curiosity. The more puzzlement and questioning becomes a habit, the more learners take it as a way of working and the more intriguing learning becomes. People are the greatest models and as a teacher we can often come into a class and start with a question that has interested us and to which we do not genuinely know the answer. Discuss why it might or might not be of interest, and how we can go about researching some answers. If a question particularly 'bites', then pose it as a family challenge, that is, something for the whole family to be involved in, for a prize at the end of term for the best solutions.

A very powerful method is the community of enquiry initiated by the philosopher Matthew Lipman. The class sits in a circle and following a stimulus, perhaps a picture book or newspaper story for example, develops philosophical questions to explore. There isn't space to develop the method here but a lot of students have found the process very engaging.

TIP:
Find out about Philosophy for Children (P4C) from www.sapere.org.uk. There are accredited training courses you can go on and, once you have been on level 1, you will see the power of the approach and be able to use it.

Application

One quick way of encouraging an approach to more open-ended questions is to build the habit of a question zone within the classroom. Have a board or piece of paper, or even a virtual space, where the headings such as these can be put up.

> 'I am still puzzled by…'
>
> 'Can we have more time on?'
>
> 'Could we improve this by…?'
>
> 'What if….?'

Encourage students to post questions through the sessions under each heading as the question strikes them or at a given time. Doing it spontaneously is best, before we forget the puzzle that was on our mind. Encourage constructive and supportive comments and model this through answering those constructive ones and taking student questions seriously. There can be a challenge to try and outwit everyone by asking the most difficult 'What if…' question related to the topic.

Concept

Visual puzzles

Puzzles can play an important part in learning. As with games, they can be used as starters, icebreakers or to give a short break after an intensive activity, and, unlike physical games, you don't need to have lots of space, or to rearrange the furniture. Doing puzzles of any sort can be a team building activity.

Puzzles don't always have to be verbal or numerical. Many students like to learn visually, so picture puzzles will appeal to them.

- As an introduction to a topic, use a pair of almost identical pictures relating to the topic and ask students to spot the differences; while they are finding them, they will be taking in any information about the topic that the picture provides.

- Spotting the mistakes in a picture is another activity worth trying; when looking at health and safety in the home or in laboratories, this could be spotting the potential hazards in a scene.

- Photographs of artefacts from unusual angles are relatively easy to take, and could provide an intriguing starter for a lesson in which the artefacts will feature.

- Completing sequences, using symbols rather than numbers or letters, will help students to gain the skill.

- A 'Quick on the Draw' game, in which students have to draw representations of book titles or names of people or objects, can provide a fun element to a topic and allow students who are more comfortable with pictures than words a chance to excel.

Application

Optical Illusions

Optical illusions, particularly those in which the observer has to find two images contained in the same picture, are fun to do and also make the point that we often have to look at things in more than one way, which could be a topic for discussion in, for example, citizenship.

Optical illusions are easy to find on the internet. As well as using them in lessons, you could try putting them up as a classroom display.

Is the curve a spiral or several lines?

How many women can you see in this picture?

How many complete triangles are there in this picture?

Is this picture possible? If not, why not?

Concept

Word games and puzzles

There are endless variations on crossword puzzles, all of which can be adapted to specific subjects and topics. Word searches are also popular, but be careful not to overuse them as students can find them repetitive. Word searches are more engaging when students have to search for the answers to questions rather than just a list of words.

There are a number of programs available for making crosswords and word searches on computers, or you could set students a task of making them up themselves and giving them to their classmates to solve. An alternative would be making up puzzles for a younger age group, which you could test on another class and report back to the makers how well their puzzles have been received.

Other types of word puzzles include 'Odd One Out' (see p49), where there may be more than one right answer and students have to justify their criteria for judging the odd one, 'A–Z Review' (see p49), making as many words as possible out of a longer word and sorting out jumbled up words.

TIP:
Word games and puzzles are available on sites such as www.funs.co.uk/wordsearch/index.htm and www.funbrain.com/detect or others on the internet. Riddles and jokes are available on www.justriddlesandmore.com or www.riddlenut.com.

Application

Riddles are another type of word puzzle, involving working out verbal clues and understanding double meanings of words, for example, 'What's black and white and red (read) all over?' (a newspaper or a book). Verbal logical puzzles often involve reasoning and identifying misdirection, for example, 'A plane crashes on the border between France and Spain. Where are the survivors buried?' (The survivors aren't buried because they are still alive.) 'A boy and his father are in a road accident. The father dies. The boy, seriously injured, is taken to hospital for an operation. The surgeon comes to the operating theatre and says, "I can't operate on this boy. He's my son." What's the explanation?' (The surgeon is the boy's mother.) Logical puzzles like these can lead to a discussion about assumptions and misinterpretations, perhaps as a preliminary to assessing evidence or texts.

Palindromes are good sources of riddles such as:

Pronounced as one letter but written with three, only two different letters are used to make me.

I'm double, I'm single, I'm black, blue and grey.

I'm read from both ends and the same either way.

Answer: EYE

Have riddles on the walls or desks for groups to ponder over as they come into a lesson. Look at how the riddles are constructed, and challenge students to come up with their own.

Concept

Logic and number puzzles

Non-verbal puzzles will be popular with students with mathematical/logical intelligence. There are plenty of examples of number puzzles around at the moment, in the shape of sudoku and its many variations. These are readily available in newspapers, books and on the internet (for example www.websudoku.com or www.dailysudoku.com/sudoku/index.shtml). Sudoku uses numbers, usually 1 to 9, but it would be possible to substitute nine different letters, perhaps the initial letters of a sequence, so that doing the sudoku would become a mnemonic. You could also substitute symbols for the numbers. Getting students to make up their own sudokus, and trying them out on each other, would also be a useful exercise.

Other number puzzles include crosswords involving numbers rather than words, with sums as the clues, and number searches, which are like word searches, with the answers to number sums and problems hidden among random numbers. Again, students could be set the task of making up their own.

Visual logic puzzles can involve finding the number of shapes in one big shape, for example, the number of triangles in one big triangle (see p83 for an example), or they can ask the observer to rearrange the shape in a seemingly impossible way. Mazes, which can be made in shapes relating to topics and subjects, are available in books and on the internet (for example www.clickmazes.com or www.logicmazes.com).

> **TIP:**
> For an interesting collection of curious puzzles, including many number ones, see David Wells' book on p96, or go to www.jimloy.com/puzz/match.htm.

Application

Crossing the River puzzles are fascinating little visual logic puzzles. The second one can be done as a role play as well.

There is a Man, a Piglet and a Fox and a Cabbage

- The boat can hold only the man and one other thing
- The fox can't be left with the pig
- The piglet can't be left with the cabbage

How do they all get across?

The Jealous Friends

- Three pairs of friends need to cross the river
- The boat holds up to three people at a time
- No friend will let their friend be in the boat or on either bank without being with them (or they might make friends with someone else and not be their best friend anymore).

What's the smallest number of boat crossings?

Desert Challenge

Thanks to Craig Roberts, a wonderful teacher in Rotherham, who devised this one to delight and challenge his students. This can be found at www.challengeclub.info. Craig said his primary school class got so intrigued by it they spent a month on the solution including making up computer simulations to help solve it.

Soldiers in your base camp on the edge of the desert desperately need medical supplies. You have to cross 600 miles of desert to get them. Your truck can carry only 400 miles of fuel including the fuel in the tank. Your base camp has a huge supply of fuel. You can make fuel dumps along the way to use for fill ups. How can you safely get across the desert and back with supplies?

The solution can be worked on with models, or on paper, or on computers so it can engage learners who like to tackle things in different ways.

Matchstick puzzles are based on logic and they also appeal to students who prefer to work kinesthetically, because there is an opportunity to move the matchsticks around. They can work as a team exercise using garden canes instead of the matchsticks. If necessary these can also be reproduced on paper and used with a pen or pencil to solve.

Concept

Games for those odd moments

Using games to engage humour and affect the energy levels of pupils can be done quite simply. Not all games entail rearranging the space in the classroom or going to a hall. It's often fun to play an impromptu game to mark the end of one activity or to provide a break after a demanding activity or to fill in a few minutes at the end of a lesson.

It's worth remembering that not all students will enjoy playing these games, and some might even find them intimidating. Always make sure the instructions are clear and that you stick to ground rules which encourage students to be supportive of each other. Try to avoid making games too competitive; in particular, don't have too many games in which participants are 'out', and, most important, play a variety of different types of games.

Application

Follow the Leader

Participants can sit at their desks or tables but they need to be able to see each other. Send one person out of the room. While they are out, pick one person in the room to be leader. Everyone else in the room has to copy everything the leader does. They should also make other movements, sounds, and so on, as a distraction. When the person outside returns, they have to guess who the leader is. They have three guesses. If they guess correctly, the leader goes out and becomes the guesser; if they don't guess correctly, they have to go out and try again.

Synchronized Stand Up

This is a seemingly simple game but can be very difficult. It's good for practising non-verbal clues and helping groups bond. It is a quick and simple energizer. The game is played in silence. Sitting in chairs so that everyone can see each other, the task is to get two people who stand up at exactly the same time, but only two. People can start whenever they want but as soon as they've stood they have to sit down again. Two people have to be synchronized.

1-2-3-4

In threes, facing each other with one fist each out. Shake fists up and down together four times while chanting '1-2-3-4' (these are the only words ever spoken). On the count of 4 each person puts out any number of fingers from 0 to 5. The object of the game is *without ever talking to each other* for the three to have exactly 11 fingers out. Once they have achieved 11 try getting to 23 using two fists.

Concept

Brain Gym®

Brain breaks are short, snappy activities that can help to energize the brain and refocus attention. They have featured in the *Guardian*'s 'Bad Science' column as some rather extravagant claims have been made on their behalf. However, many teachers swear by them. They can be useful for the beginning of a session or at any time when attention starts to flag. Sitting still for long periods of time is often difficult for children (and adults!) so brain breaks give them an opportunity to move, and break up the lesson.

Some research suggests that cross-body exercises such as Cross Crawl and Nose/Ear Change can improve co-ordination, visual, auditory and kinesthetic ability and can even improve listening, writing and memory. Some research suggests that just standing up and being more active helps by getting more oxygen to the brain. Despite questions about the research, these activities are good fun and help energize learning.

It's best to intersperse brain breaks throughout a session rather than to do them all at once, and to perform them in a slow, deliberate manner at first rather than too quickly.

Application

Some brain breaks to try.

Nose/Ear Change
Pinch your right ear lightly with your left hand and then pinch your nose lightly with your right hand. Then switch so that you are holding your left ear with your right hand and your nose with your left hand. Gradually speed up but be careful not to punch yourself.

Cross Crawl
From standing, begin to march in time. As you raise your knees, touch each one with the opposite elbow.

Doodle in the Air
With your preferred hand write out a letter. Practise different letters and then, using your other hand as well, write the mirror image of the letter. Next, try writing your whole name. If you are right handed, start in the centre and work out. If you are left handed, start at the outside and work in. You can also do this with keywords, formulae, difficult spellings and so on.

Lazy Eights
With one arm extended in front of you and your thumb pointed upwards, trace the shape of a figure of eight in the air. The eight should be on its side and, as you trace it out in large, slow movements, focus your eyes on your thumb. Without moving your head, trace three eights in successively larger movements. Now do it with your other hand and then clasp them together and do both.

or

Trace a 'lazy eight' with one hand. Then, with both hands starting in the centre, make yourself trace it in the opposite direction, so that if you start by tracing the eight with an upward movement with your right hand, you start the left hand with a downward movement.

Concept

Brain-teasers

Having a puzzling attitude towards learning is so important for young people to acquire a sense of intrinsic enjoyment and engagement with the learning process. We all need to acquire the habit of having fun with open-ended and complex problems, some of which may have more than one solution. To get into this puzzling way of thinking, it helps to create a fun and puzzling environment. There are many different forms of 'brain-teasers' and examples of visual and logical ones have already been given. Here's another interesting site to visit:
www.niehs.nih.gov/kids/braint.htm.

It's often useful to have starter activities such as puzzles or brain-teasers, on paper or card, lying on the tables when the students arrive, so that they can get on with them as soon as they sit down. These challenges have to be fairly difficult, so that the first student to arrive doesn't solve them before the rest of the class has seen them. Alternatively, put out interesting objects or pictures relating to the topic and ask the students to work out what they think they are as the rest of the class arrive. For a quick activity when all the class is there, set a time limit for the challenge.

Again overkill through the continuous use of one sort can also deaden students' enthusiasm, so use a rich variety and use with subtlety – for example, have some lying around as students come into the classroom, or create a puzzle club-time for when some work has been completed, or use as energizers in a quickfire round to alter the mood in lessons. Work in teams and give some time if necessary for the students to take home and get their families involved.

Answers: easy on the eyes, touch down, about turn, black overcoat, double time, shifting sand, hurry up, stop following me, split level, neon light, long weekend, reading between the lines, dark ages, crossroads, paradise (ouch!), split decision, tricycle, downtown, backwards glance.

Application

Count on This

Divide the group into twos or threes. Throw a die three times to get a three-digit number. Write this on the board. Ask the groups to call out three two-digit numbers and three one-digit numbers. Teams have two minutes to get as close to the large number as possible by adding, subtracting, multiplying or dividing the other six numbers. Each number can be used only once.

Brain-teasers

Set the group a brain-teaser to ponder at the start of the session, for example, *A man is pushing his car round a corner. He stops in front of a hotel and immediately knows he is bankrupt. Why?*
Answer: He is playing Monopoly™.

Sequences

Put papers on the tables or desks so that the students see them as soon as they come in. Tell them to complete the sequence and explain how they did it, for example, *The sequence is O T T F F S S E. What are the next two letters?*
Answer: N T (each letter represents the first letter of the numbers, 1 to 10, when written as words).

Can You Cut a Hole In It and Walk Through?

Take an A4 piece of paper, cut a hole in it so that you can walk through but without breaking the circumference. It is possible, we'll leave you to work it out!

The Rebus Brain-teaser (answers on p92)

EZ iiiiii	T O U C H	AB O U T	BLACK COAT
TIME TIME	S A N D	HURRY	ME STOP
LE VEL	KNEE LIGHT	W E E K E N D	
RIEIAIDIIINIGI	**AGES**	R ROAD A D	DICE DICE
DEC ISION	CYCLE CYCLE CYCLE	T O W N	ECNALG

Concept

The challenge framework

To round off the book, think about a challenge that lasts a week and puts a lot of these applications together. Learners like the idea of being challenged and it helps to model resilience, co-operation and problem-solving skills through giving them an open-ended problem or a design objective that will be difficult to solve and requires teams to work together, using everyone's strengths. These challenges take a while to put together but we know from our summer school framework that this can be time well spent because they are fun and, if planned well with a number of colleagues, make a real change from timetabled activity.

Application

This framework has been successfully used by the UFA to have fun with learning in the summer holidays. First, think of a good challenge that will engage learners; it may well come from the students themselves. Tell them they will have to present on it at the end and celebrate their achievements. Examples are building a sensory garden in the community, a research challenge in a topic area such as space or the environment. Again possibilities are only constrained by our imaginations.

1. Icebreakers and getting to know you games.
2. Games to get into teams, decide how, on rules for communicating with each other.
3. Understanding our strengths as learners (multiple intelligences, reflecting on their weaknesses as well). How do we use this knowledge in answering the challenge?
4. Understanding the challenge, plan and design how we are going to answer it.
5. Interrogate experts, seek evidence and build solutions. Represent the findings in a variety of ways such as drama, mime, song, posters, tables, diaries and so on.
6. Use visits, witnesses and experts to support.
7. Spend time for the teams to prepare a demonstration of their learning.
8. Demonstrate and CELEBRATE the learning, invite lots of people and VIPs, make a big thing of the sharing.
9. Each day should include plenty of energizers and a lot of review games so that learners are constantly refreshing where they have got to. If you have trained peer tutors who are at least two years older than their peers, they can be very helpful in designing and running the challenges.
10. If you can, have a news team to run a daily bulletin board and produce an end of challenge newspaper; this helps to contribute to the sense of fun and challenge.

Bibliography

Baldwin, P. (2004) *With Drama in Mind: real learning in imagined worlds*, Network Educational Press, Stafford

Brandes, D., Philips, H. (1979) *The Gamester's Handbook*, Nelson Thornes, Cheltenham (still available; now with two more volumes)

Caglioli, O., Harris, I. and Tindall, B. (2002) *Thinking Skills and Eye Q: visual tools for raising intelligence*, Network Educational Press, Stafford

Calvert, C. and Sikes, S. (1997) *50 Ways to Use Your Noodle: Loads of Land Games with Foam Noodle Toys*, Learning Unlimited Corporation, Tulsa (also from the same source, *50 More Ways to Use Your Noodle*)

Fisher, P., Wilkinson, I. and Leat, D. (2002) *Thinking Through History*, Chris Kington, Cambridge

Leat, D. (1998) *Thinking Through Geography*, Chris Kington, Cambridge

Northumberland County Council, Thinking For Learning

Sanders, G. (1991) *The Pictorial Guide To Group Work Activities*, published by Geoff Sanders (ISBN 0 951 7302 0 7)

UFA (2002) *Brain Friendly Revision*, Network Educational Press, Stafford

UFA (2004) *Let's Learn How to Learn*, Network Educational Press, Stafford

UFA (2004) *Helping My Child to Learn* available from www.aoy.org.uk

Wells, D. (1992) *The Penguin Book of Curious and Interesting Puzzles*, Penguin, London

Wilson, Pip and Long, Ian (2005) *Big Book of Blobs*, www.blobtree.com

Zelinski, E.J. (1998) *The Joy of Thinking Big*, Ten Speed Press, Berkeley